Renovation

Books by Jeffrey Thomson

The Halo Brace
The Country of Lost Sons
Renovation

Renovation

Poems by
Jeffrey Thomson

Carnegie Mellon University Press
Pittsburgh 2005

Acknowledgments

Grateful acknowledgment is made to the editors of the following magazines in which these poems first appeared, some in slightly different form:

Antithesis (AUS): "The Other Side"
Blue Mesa Review: "Cosmography"
Blue Moon: "Television in Another Language"
Faultline: "Light Through Glass"
Flint Hills Review: "Learning the Dead by Name," "Imaginary Numbers," "Fucking on the Confederate Dead"
Poems & Plays: "Avenue of Chance Ascent" & "My Mother's Sunflowers" (as "Ode to My Mother's Sunflowers")
Poetpourri: "Scars"
Quarterly West: "Fermata: Madison, Wisconsin," "Theft Elegy: St. Louis, Missouri, 1994" & "Autumn and Spring: Madison, Wisconsin" (as "Theft Elegy")
Whiskey Island: "Still Life with Rain and Rilke"

"Telegram to Your Old Age" is from *Biografía : poesía completa, 1958–1984*. (Anthropos, 1986) © Felix Grande.

"Scars" won the Academy of American Poets Prize (judge Robert Hass), "My Mother's Sunflowers" won First Place in The Wednesday Club of St. Louis' 63rd Annual Poetry Competition, and "Envoi" won the St. Louis Poetry Center's Open competition. "Renovation" was one of the Fellowship winners for the Writers @ Work Conference.

I want to thank Sherod Santos, Lynne McMahon, Prahlad Folly, Christopher Howell, Tony Deaton, Penelope Pelizzon, Amy Sage Webb, and Kevin Stein for their help with these poems and more importantly for their friendship in the dark hours. And thanks to Cynthia Lamb for being a kind guide, and to Jennifer and Julian, of course.

The publication of this book is supported by a grant from the Pennsylvania Council on the Arts.

Library of Congress Control Number: 2004100920
ISBN 0-88748-428-X
Copyright © 2005 by Jeffrey Thomson
All rights reserved
Printed and bound in the United States of America
Book design and composition by Richard Foerster

10 9 8 7 6 5 4 3 2 1

Contents

for Karl

. . . Bits of wreckage. Some bones. The words of the dead.

—Cormac McCarthy

Television in Another Language

Through the blue swale
of the room's small black and white,
a woman, in what must be red taffeta,

pauses in seduction—her husband's lawyer—
her breath on his neck from beneath
a veil of blond lace. There's more than this,

a fading caress; such scenes come to nothing,
blank as the emerald arch-lit hallway
which empties into the Place Nationale,

the dark shadows of cannons, shuffling
pigeons and beyond, the stairs descending
from the alley's dark cobbles

into some other tongue, gestures which slip
inside the star-dark constellation in the mirror
of a bar lined with corked bottles luminous

with pickled fish, octopus and squid,
a mirror that gives back the smoke
of a room where words choke the air,

languages in whorls above the cracked plaster,
dusted bricks, books, half-opened bottles of wine.
Remember the sunlit, glass-bricked girders,

the loaves of black bread and duck canvas counters
of the Marché St. Émelion layered with iced pike
and albacore, dripping water slipping into the sewers?

But this is Lisbon—the bar's slick tile
littered with whole fried fish, small as fingers
on greased paper plates. Behind us

in the mirror, men crowd tables to mutter
over Portugal's loss to Brazil, their talk
as old as the smoke-soaked stones.

There is a language for all this. Consonant
and vowel. Sunlight through glass and black girders.
Football under blaring halogen. Fish bathed

in cracked ice. Begin again. . . . There is a red dress.

Avenue of Chance Ascent

i.

Below the rows of towering live oaks,
  Barcelona's hash hustlers pass through
newspaper shacks and the lilt of gelato vendors
  and Las Ramblas descends to the sparkle

of the polluted Costa Brava where it splits
  like genealogy, but if you leave the trees
and walk past the flames that lick the racks
  of roasting chickens and the heavy metal

cowboys who will have, just before you pass,
  crashed the jewelry shop's plate glass
and scattered with diamonds and silver
  and handfuls of tinsel, you might see

in these streets bending back and again
  a darkness, a shadow which gathers as sound
below the window: the cough of bus exhaust,
  the rattle of bottles delivered to Café Romano,

the maid running her vacuum through
  frayed hallways and the disinterested lobby,
the chortle of doves on the balcony
  of a room where I'm curled in damp sleep,

trying to wash away the vodka I had hoped
  would ease me into the night train's sway.
I couldn't sleep in the Pyrenees where,
  outside of Andorra, the side rail held a wreck

of railcars, where the pull of explosives
  had opened and rolled the metal back into
a corolla of black petals. So I watched the dark hills
  roll into the exploding dawn, into today

where I've broken open the morning, stepping
  from a train of Paris' disregard
into Catalan's breath, husky as tar, where,
  through it's not even ten, in the plaza

drunks in high zeal whirl with fireworks
  to celebrate spring; *Festival du Printemps*
says the desk's frail man in broken French—
  our accident of a common language—

as his hands hook in his vest and he winces
  with every explosion.

ii.

Awake in the afternoon, echoing fireworks
   startle, again and again, the rock doves
who whirl in continuous curves round
   the dry fountain. Yet, it's a calm one,

I'm told. The year before, hogs ran wild
   through the quarter; a tractor-trailer
on the slaughterhouse run rolled the tight turn
   around the *Mirador de Colón*. Streets thick

with frenzied pigs and smoking steel,
   a dazed woman amazed her husband died
so easily, her blue dress charred and open
   at the throat, a gray hand dappled

with ash in a window: accident or not,
   it's the crash, the act of exploding
and every evolving opening, death's million
   possible doors which define us.

High above water, where the streets fill
   with Carnival, I hook a woman's arm
and we shout open bottles of dollar champagne
   and serpentine through penny games,

fathers with sharp tongues, the glitter
   and snatches of Spanish; the street smells
of sausage and garlic and wine; my hand
   on her neck, slender beneath

the dark savanna of her hair
   and the water of her eyes
which sparkles as fireworks thud above,
   all feathers and tufts of crimson and gold—

our ancient need to praise the rise
   of winter's survivors and consecrate
the surge of spring that expands
   and explodes as surely as it dies,

leaving only this dark and vital vacancy
   we rush again to fill.

Cosmography

There dwells in the sun simple intellect, the source,
whatsoever it may be, of every harmony.
                                        —Kepler

i. Moons

The back lawn hoary
with frost, our breath ruffles
through the black air.

The god of gods bright
in the socket,
a flattened disc

of orange and gold,
ringed by royal flecks
of light. We know

names for four
of Jupiter's twelve,
worlds too cold for desire.

All these: Io, Europa,
Ganymede, Callisto—abducted
across the star-dark ocean,

hauled close, pulled
by bull gravity. But
a few we cannot see

spin retrograde.

ii. Chaos

Kepler at his drawing table
spun music into the spheres,

ratios of major third
to perfect fifth rounded up

to the cube, dodecahedron,
and other perfect solids,

a whole cosmos of music,
a geometry rigged in sketches,

math across the page
in faultless four-four time,

nesting doll of the six
Pythagorean solids,

an armillary sphere of music
spinning its ice-crystal polyphony

through the dimensions of the Trinity.
In truth, nine planets move

in their ellipses, and Pluto
shoulders inside Neptune

once in every revolution.

iii. Sighting

In the winter of '85,
Halley's came round again,
flaring icewhite

through Aquarius,
the sun's hot wind
braiding its tail

of frozen hydrogen.
We drove through
the low-hung haze

into fallow cornfields
chocked with broken stalks,
clumped with rubble.

Veering towards perihelion
and far less than spectacular,
it smudged the dirty horizon

in the cold sockets
of our binoculars.
This our only chance

until 2062. We turned
and kissed and fell,
each holding the other

to the cold earth
until a chill slipped
between us. Silenced,

we abandoned the sky
for the car and the radio's
low love songs barely arriving

through the distance.

iv. Eurydice

She slipped away
and autumn came
early to the mountains.

Green jays fled south,
our windowed house
first rimmed with snow.

Stung to silence
by the alternate sky
and earth,

I extinguished
all the lights
and watched the stars

come out.

v. "Let the words be yours, I'm done with mine."

40 through New Mexico in a winter
of misleading light,

long stretches of asphalt,
longer stretches of sky.

The ripples of the Dead's '74 "Cassidy"
in the tinny rear speakers. Suddenly

they appear, like sunbathers,
parallel giants,

their huge faces to the sky.
Bright as ice, the aerials

of the VLA Observatory alert
for a hum,

some pattern rising
from the deep end

of the spectrum
which will be the song

of another civilization.
What arrives

is only the remaining wash
of radiation hovering quietly

at three degrees Kelvin.

vi. Coda

Tonight, our moon, full,
abruptly close,
and badly marred,

bright as the cold curve
of our frosted car
layered with wings

of ice beneath the ropes
of bare black willows.
We turn away from Jupiter,

from our planets
and stars named
for gods, our distances

measured by light.

Learning the Dead by Name

Red dogwood petals
    crush into rust-colored buds
        before they open

into heavy drops
    of spring rain, thunder
        like large black dogs.

The new house still
    odd with flushed space.
        I wander for

minutes hunting
    the dictionary, how to
        spell *dehiscence*,

that act of bursting.
    The dogs and I
        walk to the graveyard

beyond. I like coming here
    more and more,
        the glorious wreckage

of the old stones
    the small ginkgoes,
        I'm learning

the dead by name:
    every man turned
        umber with his heart's

swollen work,
     every woman bleeding
         with birth, every child

lost through the ice
     bobs up in the green earth;
         they jaunt

through their air
     like Chagall's angels, ripe,
         uncomfortable with dirt.

Three Sketches—Trinidad & Tobago

i. Man o' War Nature Preserve

The beach is rough,
the island's north coast,
a windward scoured basalt cove.
We've come to dive
but the bay is chalked
with silt so we're tucked
under a cluster of sea grape
carving up mangoes,
our knives curling saffron
from mottled rinds, tossing
the waste away. They thicken
the air with raw sugar
as they rot hot on the sand.

A Mary-blue dory swirls
rusted into the cove,
gives up three divers,
boys with masks and fins.
Minutes later they've hauled
two turtles aboard.

Across the bay,
on an exposed stone strand,
they throw out lines, bow
and stern, and toss turtles
on the rocks—we're watching
with binoculars—flippers
slapping upside down.
They open them like oysters,
long knives and leverage.

With a splash, they're back
in their boat, and we can't
decide if it's the shells or meat
they've tossed aside.

ii. Speyside

The scalloped shell
of the village curves
along the bay, rusted
shacks shelved into
the night's black hills,
lights rise up the ravines
and vanish into the chatter—
tree frogs, keening *cocricos*.
It's hard to tell what holds
this darkness in the hills,

but the yellow lights
spike the dark water
that purls past
my feet. Sparse rain
from scattered clouds,
the Southern Cross above.
In the waves sea nettles
phosphoresce, tentacles
wavering pale and pink
and violet, pulsing
with bioluminescence;
exposed in a moment
of opening, suddenly
vulnerable with hunger.

iii. The Van-Singh Cremation Ground, Gulf of Paria

A hearse beside a sizable fire,
a narrow crumble of stone
stretching out to sea,
where a farmer, dreaming,
saw land that wasn't there,
and bucket by bucket, built
what he was too poor to buy.

Long and slack, the tide
leaves slick mud that smells
of rot and fish and clings
to the mangrove roots,
my boots, and the rough
peninsula that bulges at its end.
Prayer flags limp and faded,
poles clumped in pampas lumps.
The shrine itself is cheap—
concrete broken by the ocean—
and folds in on itself, walls marked
with candle black and drippings
coat the waxy stones.

The men in rubber boots
who fish the queasy water
are suddenly uneasy;
they're unsure what duty
would bring us this far.
Onshore, a smart crowd gathers
from rusted Citroëns. Women
in dark skirts, thin men
with dark ties. Young boys
box in short white shirts.
Black smoke billows as
the body balances on the coals,
wrapped tight in white muslin.

The Postman

Tortugero, Costa Rica

Black with bars of orange and white,
wings narrow like a dragonfly's,
she follows the same path past

the false banana and tree fern, past
the gothic tangle of the strangler fig,
the heliconia's scarlet claws made

for different mouths, runs the line
of wild impatiens and Mexican heather
at the garden's edge persistent as the rain

that nightly gallops on the tin roof.
Every day, the story goes, every day
the same course. But couldn't it be

different individuals? Who's to say that
this is not a parade of identical arrivals?
That we're not broken-down

on the median of a one-way road
to a glorious city of flight hidden inside
a succession of land-fall palms and orchids,

watching a migration to the birdless city
of the butterflies, succulent and blossom
washing over a floor of rotting fruit—

musty bananas mashed to a whiskey-scented
stew—where random names its own
reward and the mail never comes.

Cursing the Sleeping World

Up all night, the geometry of light
flowing across the ceiling
with each passing car. There is
no loneliness like mine. A house
full of breathing—the dog even
sighs from the depth of his bed.
I think of rivers, the ever-receding
curve of the Orinoco, white egrets
kicking off snags, blackwater clouds
charging up the sky. Follow
the river, green funnel. Follow
the river, black channel. Follow
the thrum of the kicking 2-stroke
that becomes the sound of my wife
breathing and I am back in my room
cursing the sleeping world. Now,

back to the river but
the water is gone, poured out
into the basin of the Atlantic.
Mudflats stretch for ribboned miles.
Fish stink and pile up among
scummed deadfall, boat keels
cupped like hands in prayer
and in the deepest channel
a collection of drowned coconuts
like buried sleepers, like skulls.

Telegram to Your Old Age

Translated from the Spanish of Félix Grande

If from fear or uncertainty
this night doesn't shove the door closed—
behind it, already stripped and awake,
the prohibited woman fills with light

I swear that when you are old
one day you will see your face and memory,
and snakes that startle the mirror
will flower towards you from this story.

II

Renovation

i. The Old City, Prague, 1990

Here the astronomical clock
off Staromestske Namesti
persists its intricate swirls
of hour and moon, fragile circle
spun within the larger face
like a drafter's template:
Charles the First blinded
its architect so he could
never build another.

And here in '68, Jan Palach
set himself ablaze. Sloshing petrol
he knelt, and with the catch
of the match, folded, burning.

And that blind one, how
he must have walked, daily,
remembering how his clock
balanced—one odd window
off to the left—how the numerals
in gold leaf glowed when the sun
rose and fell with little warmth
on a woman, scarfed and creased,
selling bundles of potatoes,
small yellow apples.

He would never see
the followers of Jan Hus
throng through the streets
raising fervent dust. Or see
them broken like joists
under the Catholic purge.

When the smoke rose
across Hus and his sweat ran
thick as wax, an old woman
tossed her bundle on the pyre.
"Sancta simplicitas," was all he said.

§

Here above the rise of Victorian balconies,
concrete planters line Wenceslas Square,
circles of bare dirt and the walls of one
are coated with wax, a thick ochre-blue
spreading downhill.
                              When again,
late in 1989, people rose from their cellars,
their faces the color of gritty stone,
they planted candles by the thousand:
a ring of light splattering their dancing,
their flags of celebration. Smoke rose
and wax ran like rain.

They're a monument moored
in the Square, large, sudden
and ominous. Slick black stone
wraps Hus as his followers raise
their fists in defiance and failure.

Palach's shrine is chafed pine,
plastered with wax and dead petals,
a mark on the wall.
                              And here,
near the National, where young men
queue to haggle for western cash,
a woman, her eyes dark as char,
wants to sell me peppers, wants
to sell me apples, potatoes,
wants to sell me anything.

ii. Elegy, 1953

Say this: the bridge bent to touch
    the dirty Monongahela.
Or say, the bridge collapsed like ribs
puckering the dark lungs of water.

It is in every way the same.

There was a bridge over a river.
Red granite scarred with quartz,
old with smoke from the barges
that year-round furrowed the water

and, just above flood stage, houses
circled the valley: fading, fretworked gables
and the slouch of small barns.

A cracked plaster kitchen, his two hands
around a coffee mug. Her pinched look.
A silver radio on the refrigerator
as outside, in the shadows, the water rose.

iii. Fermata: Madison, Wisconsin

A dark Indian runner stripes the oak
risers of the stairs, and photos ascend

in brass frames, fading yellow to gray.
A stereo still plays on wooden crates of albums.

A boy slack in a chair. Sycamore and sugar maple.
This town is the same. I could have been gone

a summer. I've been gone seven years.
A comma holds this world suspended.

Still, I would reach to this boy, then seventeen,
take his hands from the stock of that .30–06.

I would say: This is what you have given me,
I have placed cups of orchids on the water,

The silence of God is God,
                              Please, stop.

There must be a way—every language
has a word for soul and, in nearly every one,

it's the sound of breath leaving the body.

iv. The Night of the Barricades, Paris, 1968

In the yellow light of rue Gay Lussac
students muster, thousands
sprawling through the breathless streets,

blocked from the Seine and the Sorbonne
by ranks of black masks, truncheons,
dogs.

They dig into the Quartier Latin: heaped cobbles
and beneath, buried yellow sand.

The barricades multiply—bricks and billboards,
scaffolding, signposts, cars. Veins of smoke lace
through the air. The wet rage of Molotov cocktails.

Dark shells, cars, flipped and burnt,
appear along the smoking morning streets.
Shattered glass, a rubble of stone.

§

In a flower shop off Montparnasse
a woman sweeps glass from the shelves.
In the broken window, the faces of her sunflowers
hunch, touched by the ashen light.

§

For long months graffiti will appear in the night:

Allons-y!
Soyons Cruel!
Courion, le vieux monde est en arrière.

Run, the old world is behind you.

v. Renovation, Berlin, 1990

Tonight Roger Waters will perform *The Wall*
on Potsdamer Platz before the ruined shadows
    of the Kaiser Wilhelm cathedral,

where Unter den Linden ends in a dust-baked field,
ends in scaffolding—
they are renovating history.
                The Brandenburg Gate
in the wind, an arched trellis of rippling cloth.

1944 and two soldiers hunker in the bomb cathedral
of Köln. Concussions in the distance. The faint patter
of rainwater on the altar.

Tables of Russian officers' hats, olive felt,
          red satin,
infantry medals pinned on a sash.

Scrap flakes of painted cement.
Hammers and chisels for rent by the hour.

They take quarter-hour sightings through the ash-wet air
and report in over the radio:

      All's clear. Clear. Clear.

Hammers ring
        across the platz,
                cement dust
frosts our arms.
        We carry stone in cupped hands.

Beneath the crowd, this killing ground,
where soldiers cut the racing backs with crosshairs.

Drinking rain
from tin cups, they talk
                of the bodies they find,
rarely
of those left behind.

Towards midnight,
                helicopters chop
        the summer air into shadowed space,

and above the tattered stars. When the show's over
we've been in the dirt for hours.

                            —for Tony

vi. Autumn and Spring: Madison, Wisconsin

ai ai legoi!

We passed the ember of a joint on the breakwater
early nights in fall; our faces occasionally amber
in the air sharp with coming snow.

Flickering on the water, lights rose along the hillside
above the dark rock jetty.

Your words, coughed out in smoke, billowed
in the haloed lights and now you hang before me,
a rasping ghost, a thought, if I had listened
when you said: *I will take my life.*
But those aren't your words; they're mine.
I have given you to them in the silence.

§

Lake Winona still frozen, and we stepped down
off the dock, into the fog, the lights,
an early night in early spring: the last damp snow
and small puddles on the ice. Out far enough,
the world goes white. In a year you'll be dead.
All that reaches us is the crack and echoing boom
of the ice breaking up out in deep water.

§

The smaller lake, Verona, cattails and redwings,
the air is warming but the water is cold.
Nothing comes from nothing. Patterned grass
washed in the wind doesn't mean you're dead,
nor the white-tail crushed against dark lindens
on the Arboretum drive. Pine needles desiccate and fall
in circles of bronze, the hyacinth, stamped with sorrow,
I placed upon the water.

vii. The Assassination of Luis Donaldo Colosio, 1994

CNN runs again and again this footage of the pistol,
      the hand rising from the crowd,
the bloody flap of skull.

Again and again, the hand rising in the smeared crowd,
      again the wisp of smoke.
Circled accomplices shoulder security
      aside. A voice crying:
I have saved Mexico.

The hand rises again. The body never falls.

viii. Theft Elegy: St. Louis, Missouri, 1994

A later friend and I drank late
that night, the dying time

of spring, before August sears the air
and in the city there is no sanctuary

but the width of starless nights.
Cars slick in the streetlights

and from a blossoming pear a mockingbird
sounded snatches of waxwing,

the cardinal's soft diphthong.
Oriole-call and birdsong beyond name

came from a space beyond flowers,
from the dark heart of that tree,

luxurious, liquid. A street emptied
by the hour and in your room

at the top of the stairs, light
suddenly blazed, blossomed

across the limestone sills. The secret
of that light fell in ashes on the grass.

ix. Envoi

It is far from certain, but perhaps,
after weeks of rain, the hills slid

into the monastery outside of Andorra—
the church steps buried nave-deep,

vespers in a silent street—all we can say
is that he has bared his head,

cowl on his shoulders, as he kicks through streets
usually filled with sausage vendors wreathed in steam

and the glassman's rapping call echoing
off the flagstones. The dark-haired daughter

of the butcher who flirts with men around
the fountain. This is not a world

at war. This world is suddenly fluid
and a girl at the Café Mallorca sipping

from a bowl of chocolate invites herself
into the poem. She looks toward us,

a black smear of wet hair across her cheek.
Her skin smells of anise and as he passes

their eyes touch. Yet what we might imagine
is the moment before the moment

of the photo, the moment of opening the door
from the flickering cloister, his shoulder

against oak, the smell of varnish and wax,
candle smoke, wool. He throws his slender frame

against the door and the earth moves a little,
the mud against the door which he barely slips through.

III

Scars

i.

Are what we are left with,
small memories like moons
in our flesh. My elbows
streaked with fat pink bands
and a web of faint lines traces
my calves, pale nets against water,
the lines of another's anger.
But I've seen some with worse,
whose reconstructed knees broken
in bonecrush games unfurl
in thick vines on their skin,
the woman at the bank who wears
long sleeves in summer.
I glimpsed the twin tracks
on her wrists when she counted
out my traveler's checks.

The cost of skin hides the ease
of peeling it away. Try it.
Shed your skin. Leave it beside
the road you've walked far from,
beside the stone garden path
where the earth is run
with nightcrawlers and beetles,
the glistening backs of centipedes.
If you slough it off and step
into the moonlight, pale and pink
and clean, they will return,
your flesh filled with air and rising.

ii.

Aquinas thought God's martyrs glowed,
bled pure white light from their scars.
His heaven glittered with their pain.
Justin's neck a ribbon of light as though
he'd swallowed the moon. His wrists gleam,
worn clean of skin by leather thongs.
Bartholomew flayed to a glorious blaze,
his whole soul alight on itself
and Sebastian's shade run through
by bright shafts that trace their flight paths out
to those who made Heaven by the back door.

iii.

One year, the pumpkins still green
on the vine, we sneaked out with knives
in our mouths, crawling through the fur
of fat leaves, the thick, sticky runners
under an October fog and the broad Harvest moon.
Sliding our blades through the tight rinds
we carved thin words in their flesh:
West High Rules! Stomp 'em Saints!
We carved the other words, words whose
power we were just beginning to understand.
When these were found we whimpered
up against our sleep all night,
our calves stitched with dried blood.

Mother culled the garden, tending our cheers
towards the street, the words spreading
pale beige and large across the autumn
turning pumpkins, their message glowing
in the headlights along rural route seven.
The others she hacked into sweet brown pie,
cold and tender, heavy with molasses
as she made us watch the eating,
huge dark mouthfuls dripping
whipped cream, white as moonlight.

Still Life with Rain and Rilke

Under a sky heavy with arriving storms,
I remember my father and his story of rain.
I've forgotten his sputtering words,
words so fragile they broke across our patio
like porcelain. So I am left with what is left:
the spatter of drops on fat leaves,
his fragile moustache, arms
like birch branches blown in a storm.

All this is as bare as what Rodin told Rilke,
and so Rilke sat in the Jardin des Plantes
watching that panther for weeks,
watching until he saw what was there
was not watching him. The ropes of muscle
loping and returning, shoulder blades pumping
like bicycling knees, a centerless center
tightened in repetition, its own
Travailler, travailler, travailler
killed the eyes Rilke had come to see.

Under the porch light your wet hair
glistened black as the lacquer
of panther fur, as we fumbled in
out of the rain, paring off Levi's
and heavy shoes, musk rising
from our revealed flesh. We fell damp
and hungry into the dark river
of each other's body.

All this has left me strangely sad,
yet it's just the panther's sadness—
his eyes cloudy with bars—and not Rilke's,
hunched on his bench, worn from the zoo,

a cold wet day molding his hands
into forms of ache and chafe.
Mine is my father's sadness,
the fragile, simple sadness of a man
searching for the words for love
as you comb the evening from your hair,
strands splayed against the window
of your bare back like dark leaves.

My Mother's Sunflowers

Railroad ties soaked in creosote
   and rows of saffron leaves
      flecked with pellets of oil.

Their edges are a singe of brown.
   From the black stacks a smoke
      assembles and spits

as they droop halfhearted
   in the gardens of Rhode Island,
      staked in cracked earth

and tied with loose twine.
   My mother tended their seeds
      solid as fists in the pith.

In salt and butter she roasted
   sheets and sheets of seeds,
      the kitchen filling with heat

until the whole gray house
   smelled yellow as petals
      and her skin shone with sweat,

her face hot with love. But
   the truth is they tasted
      like oil when we split

their shells, so we'd suck
   the salt and litter the walk
      with wet seeds. The pigeons

chortled around our porch,
   until our neighbor griped
      about the mess of birdshit

that speckled the walk and soaked
   a breadloaf in D-Con and water.
      The birds died horribly,

that's all I can say. She wept
   and the flowers, heavy with seed
      and oil-weak heeled over,

their petals flat on the dirt.
   Though I know the Egyptians
      call the soul a bird

with a human face, I couldn't
   leave the earth where she was tucked,
      her face buried in her wings.

Imaginary Numbers

$$i^2 = -1$$

As in light coming distances
in the humming blankness
from stars already shuttered
and collapsed, as in the volume
of water not in a bottle, the area
of the shadow of a missing limb.
The way winter light through
glass warms nothing. The speed
at which, on the rain-slick
leaf-scattered Kittaning Pike,
the accident doesn't happen,
the car doesn't slew and swing
out against the oncoming traffic,
the horns don't blare, glass
doesn't turn to a geometry
of pain and so she returns home
after work with the dusk
already clambering up the house,
the porch light out, haphazard
mail and the message light
flashing down the hall.

It could be that her child,
gone to stay with his father,
has called to say he loves her,
or that her husband has left her
for another man, a rodeo clown,
and she won't know whether
to be enraged or amused.
Or perhaps it's her dentist
confirming her appointment

as her cats twine between
her legs, demanding to be fed.

If possibility is the square
of experience, what can she say
of this day, its unknown grief
haunting the house, painting
the walls with its brushwork
of headlight and shadow? Would
she wish to take it to the root,
the absolute *i* on the margins
of a tertiary world? Outside,
the rain begins again and
slaps the grass, the bare limbs
of the trees scaffolding
the exponential dark.
She snaps on the light
and sees herself repeated
in the mirror, at once doubled
and inexplicably exhausted.

Light Through Glass

> When I got to my feet
> I was a glass man.
> —Paul Durcan

Shattered glass can turn asphalt to air
like the night brittle and brilliant with stars

where two men brawl, huffing white breath,
fists hard as cracked burls as they grunt

and curse in the glass air. A crowd gathers
cautiously to divide them, each speckled

with the other's silver blood, bright spit
like tiny flecks of glass. All I want

is whiskey in the dark bar beyond,
hidden under the white rattle of words

and the lights hung like glass bells.
Two women slump at a nearby table:

the woman with a baby seat on her bicycle,
the woman in purple who stumbles.

The men who join them hardly grimace
as they toss back bourbon. They drink

with glass hands, laugh with glass eyes,
glass mouths, glass teeth. Later,

they'll fold into pairs, working
their mouths around each other,

tonguing the body's light that tastes
like hot mirrors. To be alive

is to be nothing but glass, the body's
just a jar of brittle flickering

filled with all the light we dare give.
A poet with his shards of glass words.

The clutch and yearn of lovers and brawlers,
the bright flash of the connecting fist

or heart-shaped tongue. Chin, cheek, lip, jaw.
There's so much light in the mouth.

The Other Side

for Sally

i. Distant Light

Light leaked out
onto the empty chairs,
the solid, empty tables,
mopping this kitchen's
stainless gleam,
a green glass bottle of beer
on the silver table.

Cold air arched
above the hills
where stoned Snow Cat
drivers rumbled
the slopes skiable,
their lights lifting
up stiff pitches,
disappearing into fir
as my boots squeaked
into the parking lot.
I knew you waited
in yellow light,
folded into the low
cavern of our bed
reading Dostoyevsky,
as I waited for the glow
of the bus rolling through turns,
Tuck slinging the wheel.

ii. Telemarking

Have I remembered
correctly the taste
of your hands,

the smell of butter
in your smoke-
stained hair?

The turns you taught me,
dropping my knee,
uphill arm pulled

in hard, that perfect carve?
You thought I taught
myself, each edge

slipping again and again
until finally the gentle curve
of the ski followed.

iii. Red Lady

When you left the door
open, our house of angles,

plants and sunlight bleeding
its heat into the brittle air

and walked out into the snow,
I knew you wanted to leave.

So later, as if craving
avalanche, I slipped on skins

and crossed the paths we'd worn
hip-deep in the drifts

and climbed into the moon-
bright night, the soft shush

of skis up the trails
worn into Kebler,

through sterling aspens,
groves of dark larch,

their shadows across
reclining slopes of snow,

a reminder how loss
is so closely tied to gain.

The curving edge of the cornice
above Red Lady Bowl,

the town squared far below in stripes
of yellow light. Finally falling

through huge sweeps of snow,
billows and rolls, hissing white,

washing up my chest. My skis appeared
and disappeared like dolphins.

Esses halved that bright expanse
below the black-rimmed shoulder

of the bowl, divided the world
into sides, choices—

the thing that wrecks us all.

The Affair

When Anna Karenina steps
from the radiant train
into the dark and the wind

that thrashes her, we know
it is desire we see, the body
rising up within the body

as my cock rises under
the hand of this girl, her sex
cupped in my palm. The way

sunlight rises up the wall,
the way I kiss her again and
taste the grit of her tongue

on mine as the maid thumps
her vacuum down the hall.
We let a Spaniard take us

up the coast of the Cinque Terre,
Italy's hill country come down
to kneel between the thighs

of the sea. The small dinghy
cutting across the striped lights
of Riomaggiore, their dazzle

drizzled onto the bronze flank
of the dark. It was only
on the return that we moved

together in the bow. The boat
chuffed into the harbor,
roads rising into a *purgatorio*

of windows shuttered against
the night air. Carcasses of boats
overturned on the quay.

The smell of bread in her hair.
It's all here, in pieces perhaps,
the gilded dark, trains tearing

at the hillsides with their
greased whistles. This girl
and I above the bakery. Stars

turning wheels above our heads.

Fucking on the Confederate Dead

> *Shall we take the act*
> *To the grave?*
> —Allen Tate

Summer is the adulation of the moon
on her bare breasts, my mouth on the moon,
her hand on my cock with the grass cold
and wet beneath us. The brute curiosity
of her hair curtains off my face, though
tonight the headstones are tables overflowing
with everything our separate pasts desire,
the fragrance of it on the air—wet roses,
ashes, oil—as deer hop the wall and ghost
around the stones in earshot of our sounds,
the soft Morse of secret pleasure. Headlights
bare above our bodies the trees and stones
dissolving day by day and I enter
her white flesh, enter a meadow of sighs.

You hear the shout, the crazy hemlocks point,
the rocks relax somewhat of their hardness.
The oaks lean in and willows circle us
within the green effervescence of their hair.

"Who was it you called for?"
Her reply before she kisses me again
is world weary, a tenuous grace note—
Oh, it's a long story. One you've heard before.

No time now for that last story, no time
for Orpheus and the croaking dactyls
of his unremitting grief. And, honestly,
what could he say to ease your mind?
Such narratives demand renovation, so

turn your eyes from the immodest present
and all the bodies exhausting each other
on the rain-wet grass, the melting stones.
Leave the suspiration of the earth, the chuffing
deer. Gather together the dark hours. Start now.

Notes

Avenue of Chance Ascent

Since 1983, after the failure of negotiations with the Spanish government to obtain the independence of the Basque province, the members of the Basque Separatist organization have specialized in attacking sites visited by Spanish tourists.

Renovation

i. The Old City, Prague, 1990

Staromestske Namesti is the center of Prague's cultural and historical life. In the center of the square sits the monument to Jan Hus, a church reformer burned in 1415 by the Holy Roman Emperor for heresy. "Sancta simplicitas" can be translated ironically as "Holy Fool."

In 1969, Jan Palach, then a student of aesthetics at Charles University, doused himself in gasoline and set himself on fire to protest the occupation of Czechoslovakia by Warsaw Pact forces and the abandonment of democracy by Czechoslovak politicians.

iv. The Night of the Barricades, Paris, 1968

On the evening of May 10, 1968, students and striking teachers organized a large march to demand freedom for five university and high-school students, activists in the movement against the war in Vietnam. When the demonstration reached the Sorbonne, it was already surrounded by police. After a few clashes, barricades went up throughout the Latin Quarter of Paris. The police attacked, using truncheons and chlorine gas. By early the next morning, the last barricade had been breached.

vi. Autumn and Spring: Madison, Wisconsin

Hyacinthus, they say, was a very handsome young man. Apollo fell in love with him and, in flirtatious sport, they held a contest with the discus. But when Hyacinthus ran out to catch the discus that Apollo had thrown, it struck him down. Apollo tried to save his life, but the wound was past all cure. From Hyacinthus' blood sprung a flower—the hyacinth—and its petals carry the marks of the god's grief. As Ovid says, Apollo inscribed in its petals *ai ai legoi*, which imitates the god's suffering.

vii. The Assassination of Luis Donaldo Colosio, 1994

Luis Donaldo Colosio was a Mexican politician and social development secretary under President Carlos Salinas de Gortari before resigning to run for Mexican president. Colosio was assassinated while campaigning in 1994.

Still Life with Rodin and Rilke

"Travailler, rien que travailler," Rodin answered Rilke when the poet asked the sculptor to define art. In 1905 Rilke moved to Meudon, France, to take a job as Rodin's secretary. When Rilke told Rodin that he had not been able to work, Rodin told him to go to the zoo (*le Jardin des Plantes*).

Imaginary Numbers

An "imaginary number" is a multiple of a quantity called "i" which is defined by the property that i squared equals -1. In other words, i equals the square root of -1.

Fucking on the Confederate Dead

Orpheus was inconsolable after losing Eurydice a second time. "Seven days Orpheus lingered about the brink, without food or sleep. . . he sang his complaints to the rocks and mountains, melting the hearts of tigers and moving the oaks from their stations. He held himself aloof from womankind, dwelling constantly on the recollection of his sad mischance." (Bullfinch)

You hear the shout . . . This and several other lines have been adapted from Allen Tate's poem, "Ode to the Confederate Dead."